Writing Practice for Kids

Women in History Workbook
Practice writing sentences.

Women from US History
Nancy Johnson
☐ Read the facts.

Women from US History
Dorothea

Women from US History
Ruth Mosko Handler
☐ Read the facts.
Pronouns: she/her
born in 1916

Women from US History
Wilma Rudolph
☐ Read the facts.
Pronouns: she/her
was born in 1940
died in 1994

had polio as a child
wore a leg brace as a child
was a track and field star

Write about th

Write about the person using comp

Write about th

Write about the person using complete sentences.

Capital letter | Has

I0458536

Learn about 35 women from throughout American history.

In this workbook you will learn about the contributions of women in US History from the 1700s until the 1900s. On the first page of each person, you will read facts about each person. Then there is space for you to write sentences about that person. After you write about the person go back and use the sentence writing checklist to make sure that you have written you best sentences. Then on the next page write about the same person using your best handwriting.

Mary Dixon Kies	Tabitha Babbitt	Betsey Metcalf Baker	Sacagawea	Almira Hart Lincoln Phelps	Nancy Johnson	Orra White Hitchcock
Margaretta Hare Morris	Maria Mitchell	Elizabeth Jennings Graham	Anna Dormitzerwas	Mary Harris Jones	Josephine Cochran	Emily Warren Roebling
Annie Smith Peck	Nellie Bly	Dr Susan La Fleshce Picotte	Minnie M. Cox	Tye Leung Schulze	Alice Augusta Ball	Bessie Coleman
Dorothea Lange	Dr. Mabel Ping-Hua Lee	Amelia Earhart	Margaret Hamilton	Margaret Bourke-White	Ruth Mosko Handler	Marion Donovan
Katherine Johnson	Constance Baker Motley	Stephanie Kwolek	Alice Coachman	Dr. Nancy Roman	Wilma Rudolph	Sonia Sotomayor

American Women to Read and Write About

Mary Dixon Kies 1752-1837

Tabitha Babbitt 1779-1853

Betsey Metcalf Baker 1786-1867

Sacagawea 1788-1812 or 1884

Almira Hart Lincoln Phelps 1793 1884

Nancy Johnson 1794-1890

Orra White Hitchcock 1796-1863

Margaretta Hare Morris 1797-1867

Maria Mitchell 1818 1889

Elizabeth Jennings Graham 1827-1901

Anna Dormitzerwas 1830-1903

Mary Harris Jones "Mother Jones" 1837-1930

Josephine Cochrane 1839-1913

Emily Warren Roebling 1843-1903

Annie Smith Peck 1850-1935

Nellie Bly 1864-1922

Dr Susan La Fleshce Picotte 1865-1915

Minnie M. Cox 1869-1933

Tye Leung Schulze 1887-1972

Alice Augusta Ball 1892 1916

Bessie Coleman 1892-1926

Dorothea Lange   1895-1965

Dr. Mabel Ping-Hua Lee 1896-1966

Amelia Earhart 1897 -1937?

Margaret Hamilton 1902- 1985

Margaret Bourke-White 1904–1971

Ruth Mosko Handler 1916-2002

Marion Donovan 1917-1998

Katherine Johnson 1918-2020

Constance Baker Motley 1921-2005

Stephanie Kwolek 1923-2014

Alice Coachman 1923-2014

Dr. Nancy Roman 1925-2018

Wilma Rudolph 1940-1994

Sonia Sotomayor 1954-current

Sentence Writing

- Start each sentence with a capital letter.
- A sentence has a subject. This is who or what the sentence is about.
- A sentence has an action, it is also called the predicate. This tells what is happening in the sentence.
- Check your sentences for correct spelling.
- A sentence needs punctuation marks. A sentence ends with either a period, question mark, or explanation mark.

.	?	!

The dog | ran in the yard.

subject

action

Capital letter

Punctuation

Pronouns

A pronoun takes the place of a noun.

Singular

I	me
you	you
he	him
she	her
they	them
it	it

masculine (he, him)
feminine (she, her)
gender neutral (they, them)
object (it, it)

Singular Possessive

my	mine
your	yours
his	his
her	hers
their	theirs
its	its

masculine (his, his)
feminine (her, hers)
gender neutral (their, theirs)
object (its, its)

Mary Dixon Kies

📖 **Read the facts.**

Pronouns: she/her

was born in 1752

died in 1837

was an inventor

was the first women to receive a U.S patent

created a way to weave straw with silk to use in hats.

✏️ **Write about the person using complete sentences.**

_____

_____

_____

_____

_____

_____

Sentence Writing Checklist

Capital letter	Has a subject	Has an action	Spelling	Punctuation
☐	☐	☐	☐	☐

Mary Dixon Kies

_____

_____

_____

_____

_____

_____

_____

_____

_____

Tabitha Babbitt

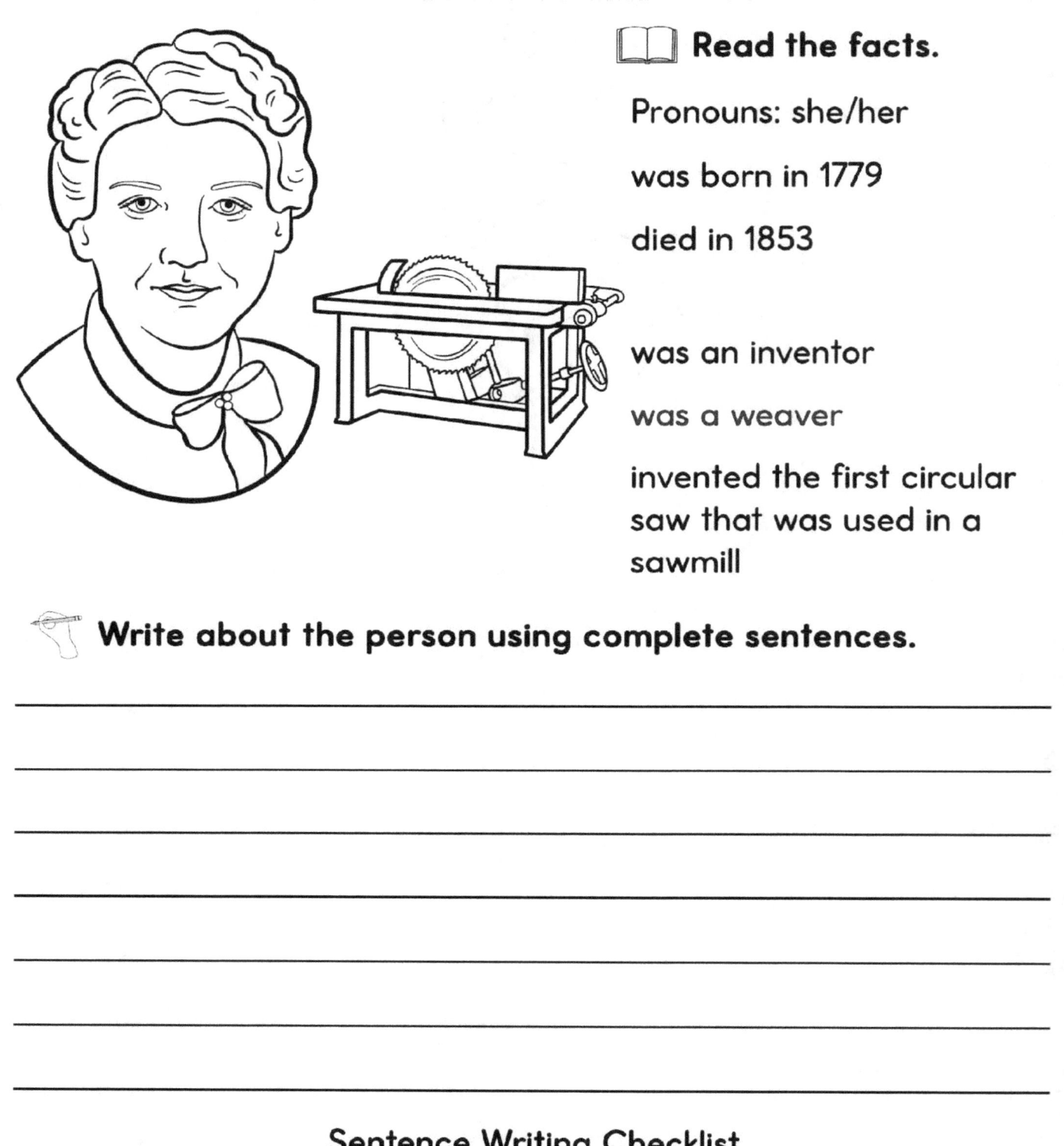

📖 **Read the facts.**

Pronouns: she/her

was born in 1779

died in 1853

was an inventor

was a weaver

invented the first circular saw that was used in a sawmill

✏️ **Write about the person using complete sentences.**

_____

_____

_____

_____

_____

_____

Sentence Writing Checklist

Capital letter	Has a subject	Has an action	Spelling	Punctuation
☐	☐	☐	☐	☐

Tabitha Babbitt

_____

_____

_____

_____

_____

_____

_____

_____

_____

Betsey Metcalf Baker

📖 **Read the facts.**

Pronouns: she/her

was born in 1786

died in 1867

was an inventor

created a new way to braid straw for bonnets

worked to end slavery

Write about the person using complete sentences.

_____

_____

_____

_____

_____

_____

Sentence Writing Checklist

Capital letter	Has a subject	Has an action	Spelling	Punctuation
☐	☐	☐	☐	☐

Betsey Metcalf Baker

_____

_____

_____

_____

_____

_____

_____

_____

_____

Sacagawea

📖 **Read the facts.**

Pronouns: she/her

was born in 1788

died in 1812 or 1884

was an interpreter

was a guide for Luis and Clark

was a mother

✏️ **Write about the person using complete sentences.**

_____

_____

_____

_____

_____

_____

Sentence Writing Checklist

Capital letter	Has a subject	Has an action	Spelling	Punctuation
☐	☐	☐	☐	☐

Sacagawea

_____

_____

_____

_____

_____

_____

_____

_____

Almira Hart Lincoln Phelps

📖 **Read the facts.**

Pronouns: she/her

was born in 1793

died in 1884

was a teacher

was a mother

wrote a botany textbook

✏️ **Write about the person using complete sentences.**

_____

_____

_____

_____

_____

_____

Sentence Writing Checklist

Capital letter	Has a subject	Has an action	Spelling	Punctuation
☐	☐	☐	☐	☐

Almira Hart Lincoln Phelps

_____

_____

_____

_____

_____

_____

_____

_____

_____

Nancy Johnson

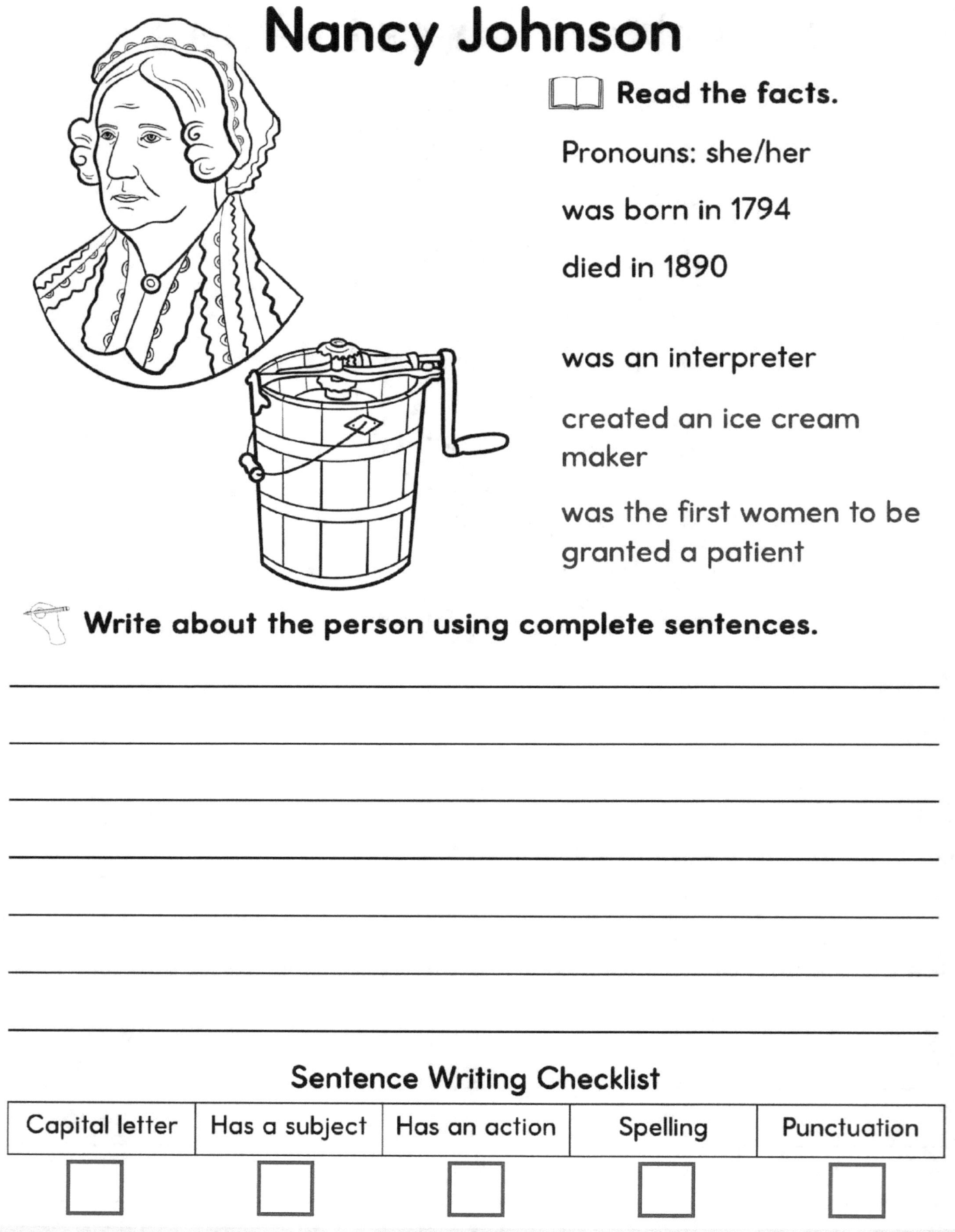

📖 **Read the facts.**

Pronouns: she/her

was born in 1794

died in 1890

was an interpreter

created an ice cream maker

was the first women to be granted a patient

Write about the person using complete sentences.

_____

_____

_____

_____

_____

_____

Sentence Writing Checklist

Capital letter	Has a subject	Has an action	Spelling	Punctuation
☐	☐	☐	☐	☐

Nancy Johnson

Orra White Hitchcock

📖 **Read the facts.**

Pronouns: she/her

was born in 1796

died in 1863

was a teacher

was a science illustrator

had six children

✏️ **Write about the person using complete sentences.**

_____

_____

_____

_____

_____

_____

Sentence Writing Checklist

Capital letter	Has a subject	Has an action	Spelling	Punctuation
☐	☐	☐	☐	☐

Orra White Hitchcock

_____

_____

_____

_____

_____

_____

_____

_____

_____

Margaretta Hare Morris

📖 **Read the facts.**

Pronouns: she/her

was born in 1796

died in 1863

caught and studies insects

was an entomologist

wrote articles for
agriculture magazines

✏️ **Write about the person using complete sentences.**

_____

_____

_____

_____

_____

_____

Sentence Writing Checklist

Capital letter	Has a subject	Has an action	Spelling	Punctuation
☐	☐	☐	☐	☐

Margaretta Hare Morris

Maria Mitchell

📖 **Read the facts.**

Pronouns: she/her

was born in 1818

died in 1886

first female astronomer in the US

was the first American scientist to discover a comet

was the first female astronomy professor

Write about the person using complete sentences.

_____

_____

_____

_____

_____

_____

Sentence Writing Checklist

Capital letter	Has a subject	Has an action	Spelling	Punctuation
☐	☐	☐	☐	☐

Maria Mitchell

_____

_____

_____

_____

_____

_____

_____

_____

_____

Elizabeth Jennings Graham

📖 **Read the facts.**

Pronouns: she/her

was born in 1827

died in 1901

was a teacher

successfully challenged racist streetcar policies in New York City

was a mother

✏️ **Write about the person using complete sentences.**

_____

_____

_____

_____

_____

_____

Sentence Writing Checklist

Capital letter	Has a subject	Has an action	Spelling	Punctuation
☐	☐	☐	☐	☐

Elizabeth Jennings Graham

Anna Dormitzerwas

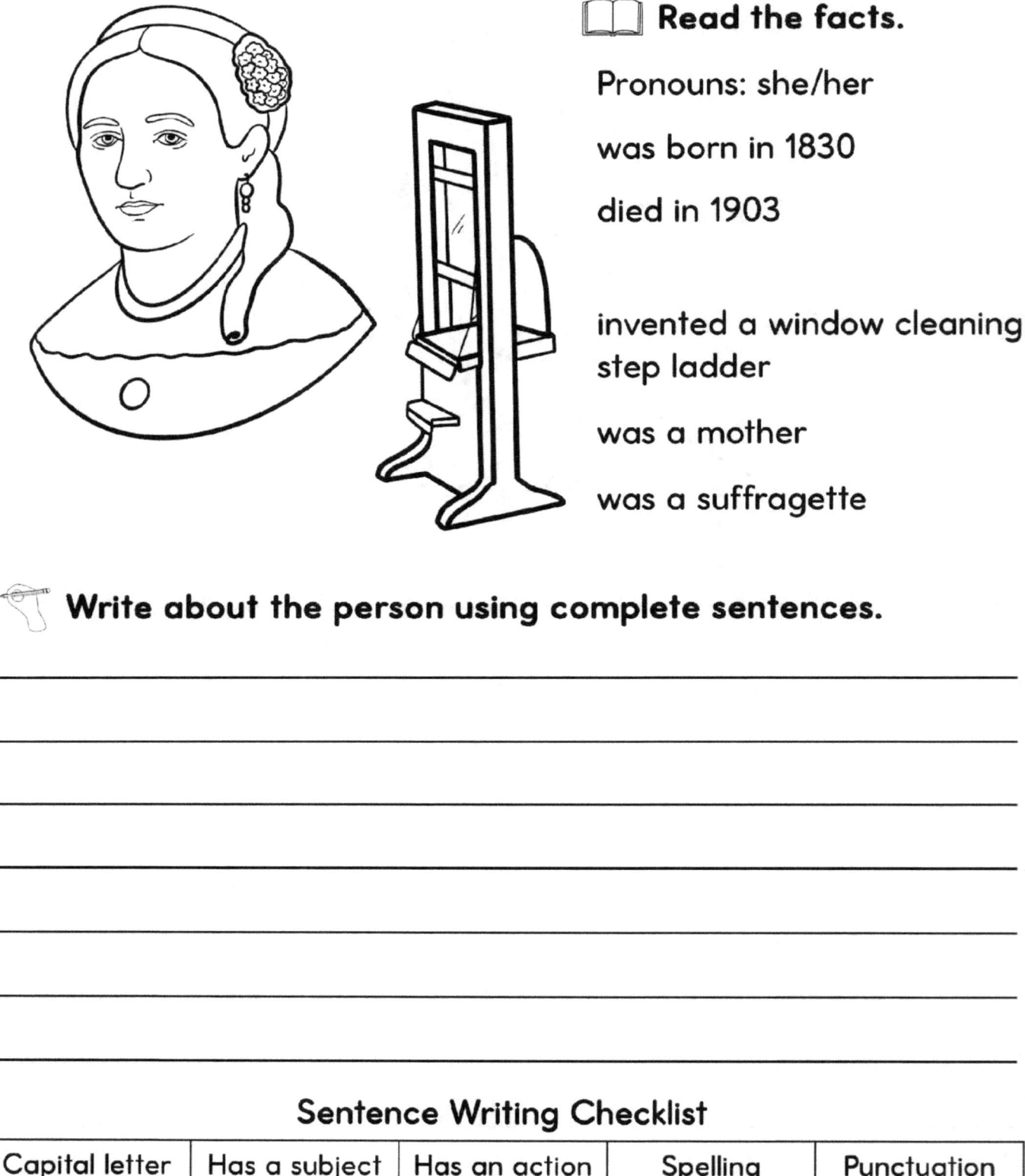

📖 **Read the facts.**

Pronouns: she/her

was born in 1830

died in 1903

invented a window cleaning step ladder

was a mother

was a suffragette

✏️ **Write about the person using complete sentences.**

_____

_____

_____

_____

_____

_____

Sentence Writing Checklist

Capital letter	Has a subject	Has an action	Spelling	Punctuation
☐	☐	☐	☐	☐

Anna Dormitzerwas

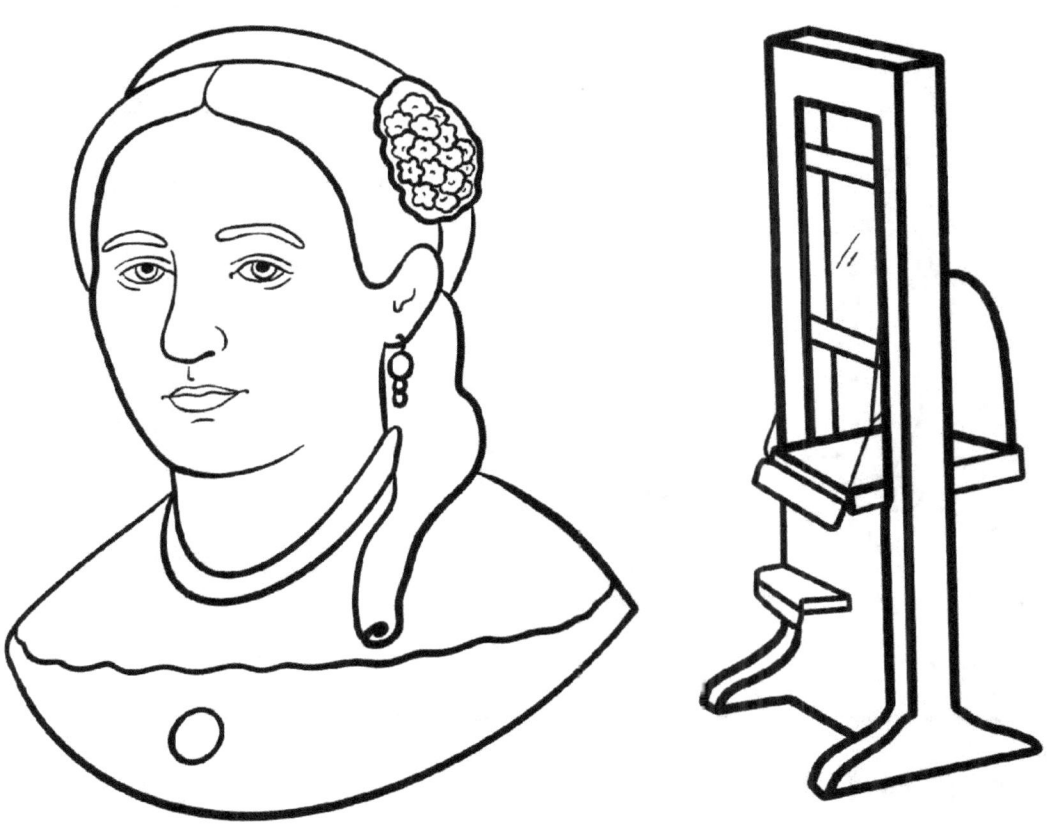

_____

_____

_____

_____

_____

_____

_____

_____

_____

Mary Harris Jones "Mother Jones"

📖 **Read the facts.**

Pronouns: she/her

was born in 1837

died in 1930

immigrated to North America from Ireland

was a seamstress

active in the labor movement

✏️ **Write about the person using complete sentences.**

_____

_____

_____

_____

_____

_____

Sentence Writing Checklist

Capital letter	Has a subject	Has an action	Spelling	Punctuation
☐	☐	☐	☐	☐

Mary Harris Jones "Mother Jones"

_____

_____

_____

_____

_____

_____

_____

_____

_____

Josephine Cochran

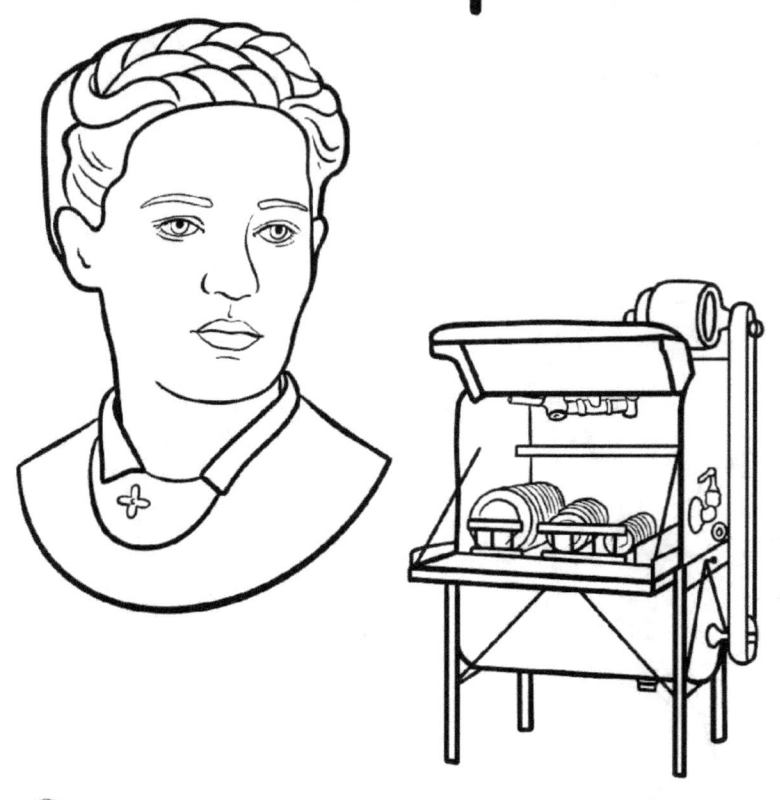

📖 **Read the facts.**

Pronouns: she/her

was born in 1839

died in 1913

was a mother

invented the first commercial dishwasher

ran Cochran's Crescent Washing Machine Company

✏️ **Write about the person using complete sentences.**

_____

_____

_____

_____

_____

_____

Sentence Writing Checklist

Capital letter	Has a subject	Has an action	Spelling	Punctuation
☐	☐	☐	☐	☐

Josephine Cochran

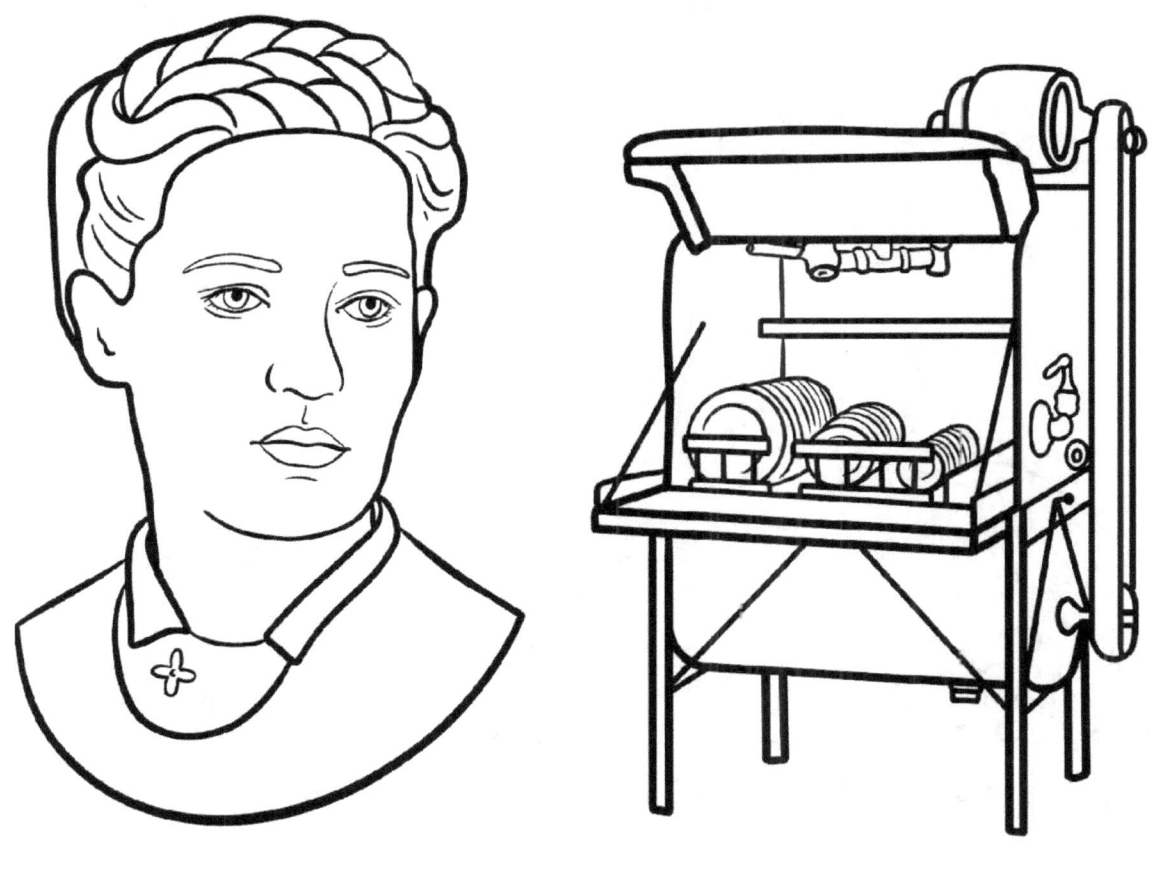

_____

_____

_____

_____

_____

_____

_____

_____

_____

Emily Warren Roebling

📖 **Read the facts.**

Pronouns: she/her

was born in 1843

died in 1903

oversaw the construction of the Brooklyn Bridge

was the first female field engineer

earned a law degree

✏️ **Write about the person using complete sentences.**

_____

_____

_____

_____

_____

_____

Sentence Writing Checklist

Capital letter	Has a subject	Has an action	Spelling	Punctuation
☐	☐	☐	☐	☐

Emily Warren Roebling

_____

_____

_____

_____

_____

_____

_____

_____

Annie Smith Peck

📖 **Read the facts.**

Pronouns: she/her

was born in 1850

died in 1935

was a college professor

teaching Latin, elocution and archaeology

summited the Matterhorn in the Swiss Alps wearing pants
was a suffragette

 Write about the person using complete sentences.

_____

_____

_____

_____

_____

_____

Sentence Writing Checklist

Capital letter	Has a subject	Has an action	Spelling	Punctuation
☐	☐	☐	☐	☐

Annie Smith Peck

_____

_____

_____

_____

_____

_____

_____

_____

_____

_____

Nellie Bly

📖 **Read the facts.**

Pronouns: she/her

was born in 1864

died in 1922

was a journalist

went undercover as a patient at a New York City mental health asylum

traveled around the world

✏️ **Write about the person using complete sentences.**

_____

_____

_____

_____

_____

_____

Sentence Writing Checklist

Capital letter	Has a subject	Has an action	Spelling	Punctuation
☐	☐	☐	☐	☐

Nellie Bly

_____

_____

_____

_____

_____

_____

_____

_____

Dr Susan La Fleshce Picotte

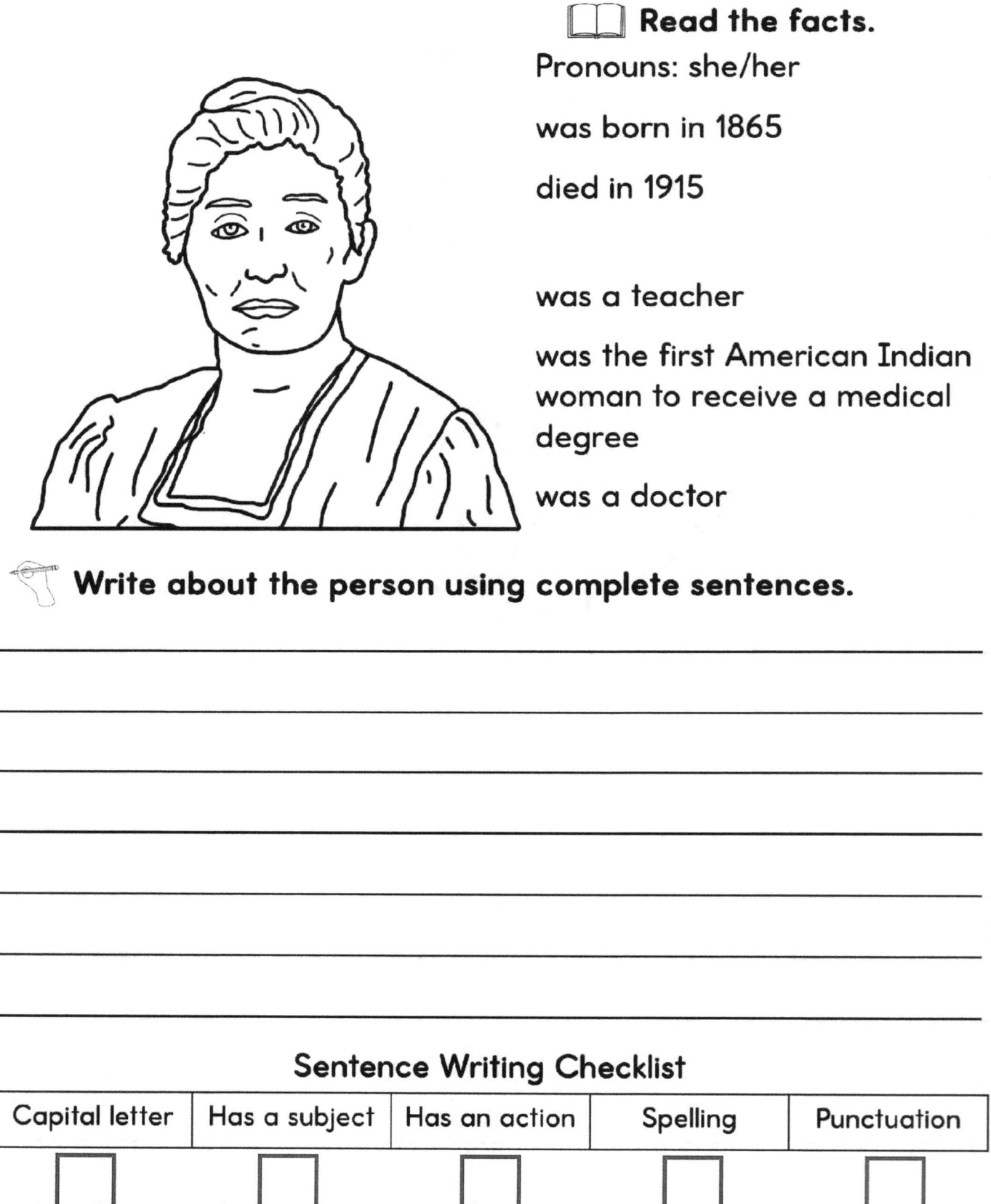

📖 **Read the facts.**

Pronouns: she/her

was born in 1865

died in 1915

was a teacher

was the first American Indian woman to receive a medical degree

was a doctor

✏️ **Write about the person using complete sentences.**

_____

_____

_____

_____

_____

_____

Sentence Writing Checklist

Capital letter	Has a subject	Has an action	Spelling	Punctuation
☐	☐	☐	☐	☐

Dr Susan La Fleshce Picotte

_____

_____

_____

_____

_____

_____

_____

_____

_____

Minnie M. Cox

📖 **Read the facts.**

Pronouns: she/her

was born in 1869

died in 1933

was a teacher

was the first African American woman postmaster of Mississippi

was a mother

✏️ **Write about the person using complete sentences.**

_____

_____

_____

_____

_____

_____

Sentence Writing Checklist

Capital letter	Has a subject	Has an action	Spelling	Punctuation
☐	☐	☐	☐	☐

Minnie M. Cox

Tye Leung Schulze

📖 **Read the facts.**

Pronouns: she/her

was born in 1887

died in 1872

was the first Chinese woman employed by the federal government

was the first Chinese woman to vote in the US

was a community advocate

✏️ **Write about the person using complete sentences.**

_____

_____

_____

_____

_____

_____

Sentence Writing Checklist

Capital letter	Has a subject	Has an action	Spelling	Punctuation
☐	☐	☐	☐	☐

Tye Leung Schulze

Alice Augusta Ball

📖 **Read the facts.**

Pronouns: she/her

was born in 1892

died in 1916

was the first woman and first African American to get a master's degree from the University of Hawaii

developed a treatment for leprosy

was the first female chemistry professor at the University of Hawaii

✏️ **Write about the person using complete sentences.**

_____

_____

_____

_____

_____

_____

Sentence Writing Checklist

Capital letter	Has a subject	Has an action	Spelling	Punctuation
☐	☐	☐	☐	☐

Alice Augusta Ball

_____

_____

_____

_____

_____

_____

_____

_____

Bessie Coleman

📖 **Read the facts.**

Pronouns: she/her

was born in 1892

died in 1926

was a single mother

was the first American woman to obtain an international pilot's license

started a school to train African American aviators

✏️ **Write about the person using complete sentences.**

_____

_____

_____

_____

_____

_____

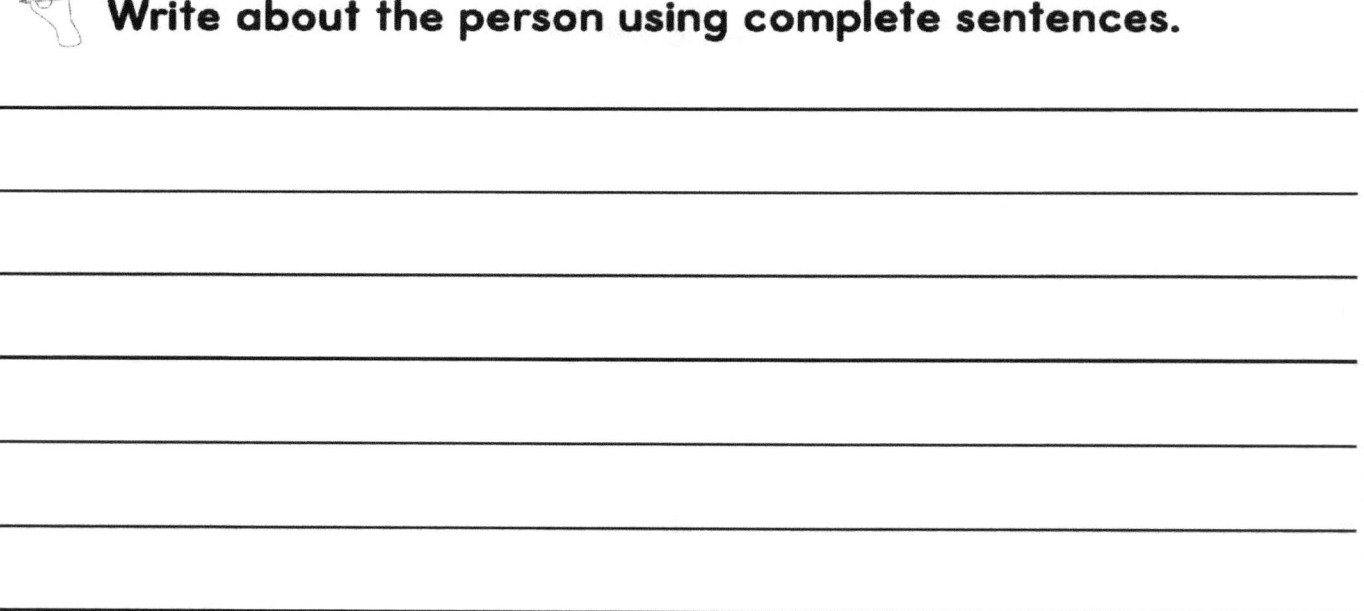

Sentence Writing Checklist

Capital letter	Has a subject	Has an action	Spelling	Punctuation
☐	☐	☐	☐	☐

Bessie Coleman

Dorothea Lange

📖 **Read the facts.**

Pronouns: she/her

was born in 1895

died in 1965

was a photographer

wanted her photographs to cause social change

photographed the incarceration of Japanese Americans in protest

✏️ **Write about the person using complete sentences.**

_____

_____

_____

_____

_____

_____

Sentence Writing Checklist

Capital letter	Has a subject	Has an action	Spelling	Punctuation
☐	☐	☐	☐	☐

Dorothea Lange

Dr. Mabel Ping-Hua Lee

📖 **Read the facts.**

Pronouns: she/her

was born in 1896

died in 1966

worked for women's suffrage

earned a PhD in economics

founded a Chinese community center

Write about the person using complete sentences.

_____

_____

_____

_____

_____

_____

Sentence Writing Checklist

Capital letter	Has a subject	Has an action	Spelling	Punctuation
☐	☐	☐	☐	☐

Dr. Mabel Ping-Hua Lee

Amelia Earhart

📖 **Read the facts.**

Pronouns: she/her

was born in 1897

may have died in 1937

was the first woman to cross the Atlantic by plane as a passenger

was the first woman to fly solo across the Atlantic

tried to fly around the world

✏️ **Write about the person using complete sentences.**

_____

_____

_____

_____

_____

_____

Sentence Writing Checklist

Capital letter	Has a subject	Has an action	Spelling	Punctuation
☐	☐	☐	☐	☐

Amelia Earhart

Margaret Bourke-White

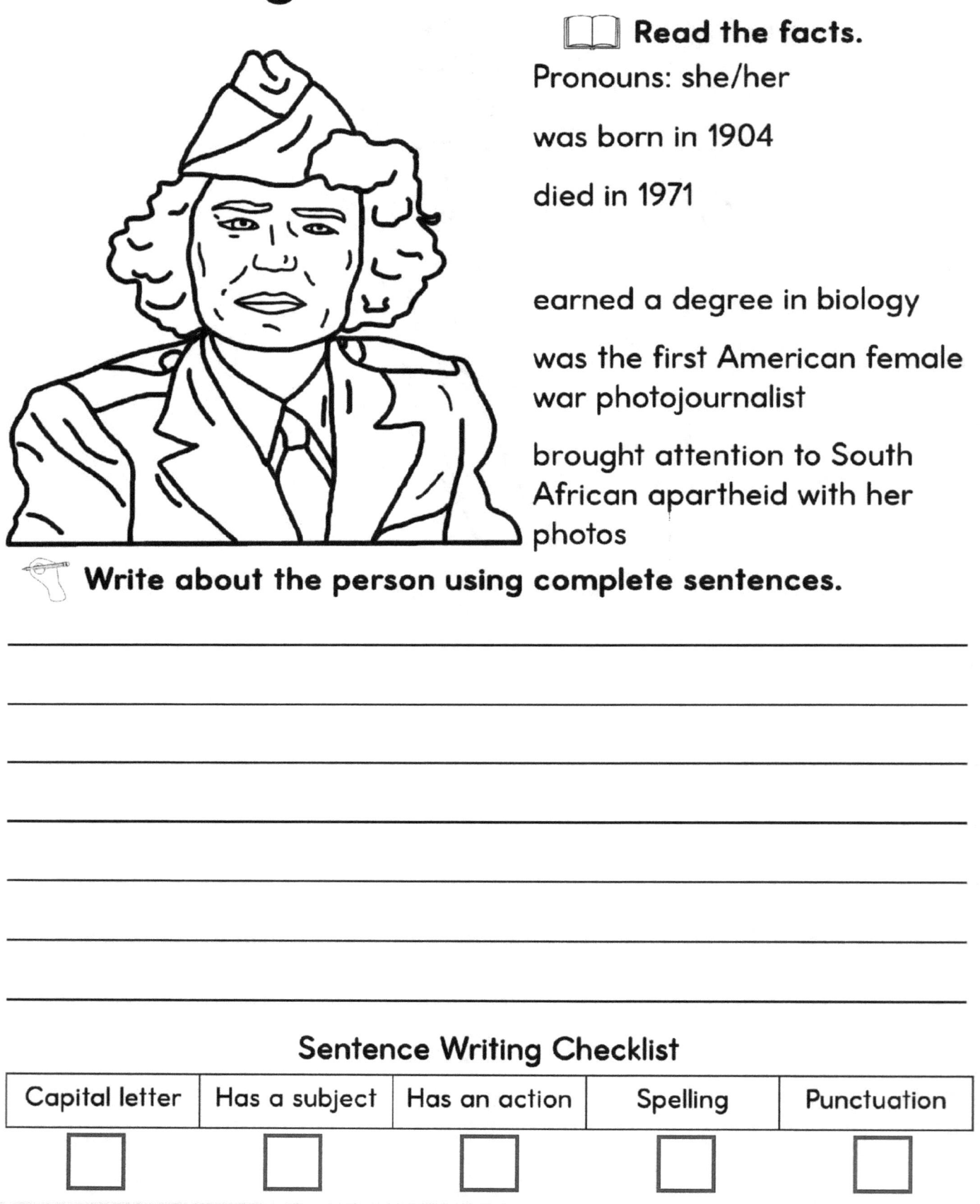

📖 **Read the facts.**

Pronouns: she/her

was born in 1904

died in 1971

earned a degree in biology

was the first American female war photojournalist

brought attention to South African apartheid with her photos

Write about the person using complete sentences.

_____

_____

_____

_____

_____

_____

Sentence Writing Checklist

Capital letter	Has a subject	Has an action	Spelling	Punctuation
☐	☐	☐	☐	☐

Margaret Bourke-White

Ruth Mosko Handler

📖 Read the facts.

Pronouns: she/her

was born in 1916

died in 2002

was a mother

created the Barbie doll

inducted into the Toy Industry Hall of Fame

Write about the person using complete sentences.

_____

_____

_____

_____

_____

_____

Sentence Writing Checklist

Capital letter	Has a subject	Has an action	Spelling	Punctuation
☐	☐	☐	☐	☐

Ruth Mosko Handler

Marion Donovan

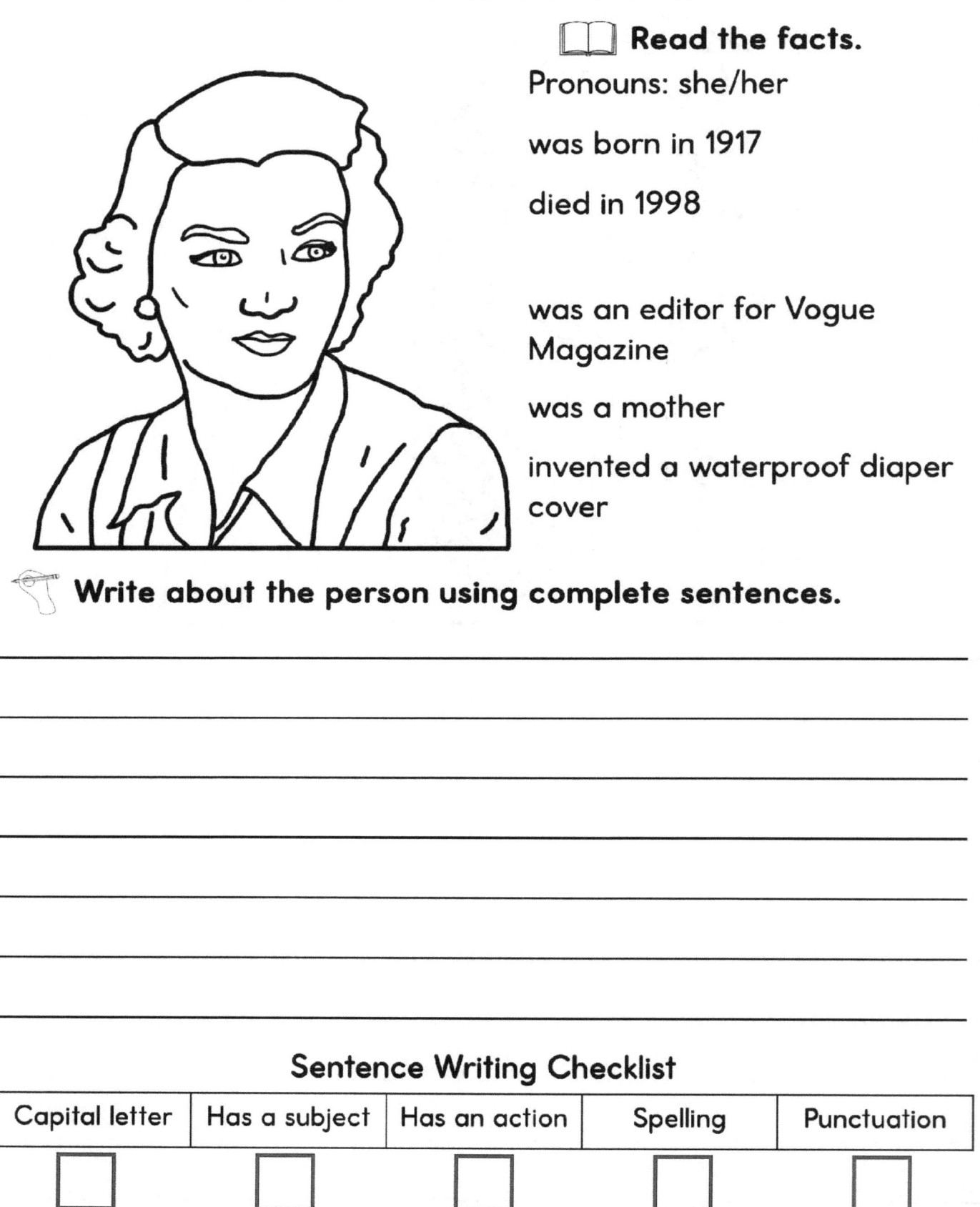

📖 **Read the facts.**

Pronouns: she/her

was born in 1917

died in 1998

was an editor for Vogue Magazine

was a mother

invented a waterproof diaper cover

Write about the person using complete sentences.

_____

_____

_____

_____

_____

_____

Sentence Writing Checklist

Capital letter	Has a subject	Has an action	Spelling	Punctuation
☐	☐	☐	☐	☐

Marion Donovan

Katherine Johnson

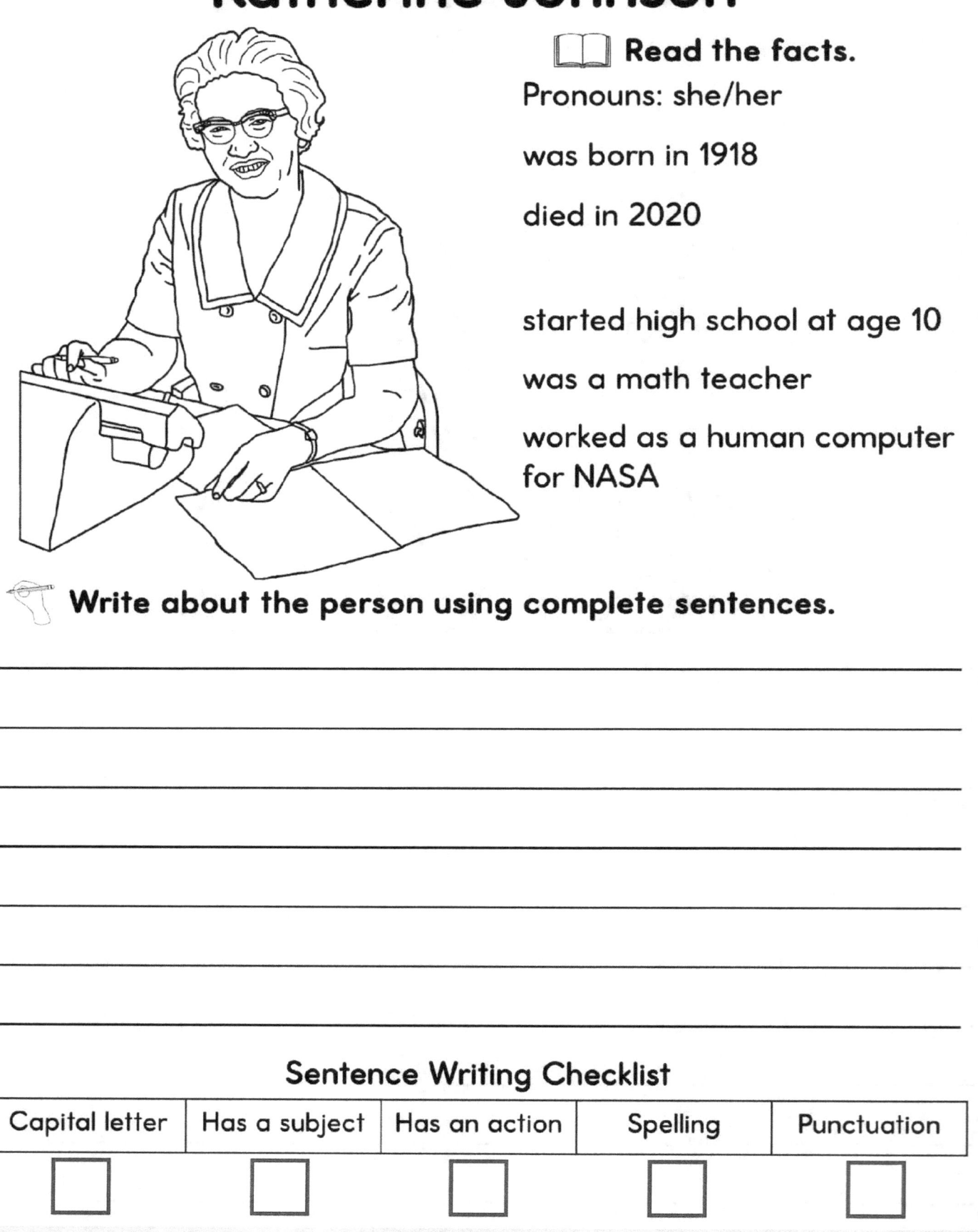

📖 **Read the facts.**

Pronouns: she/her

was born in 1918

died in 2020

started high school at age 10

was a math teacher

worked as a human computer for NASA

Write about the person using complete sentences.

_____

_____

_____

_____

_____

_____

Sentence Writing Checklist

Capital letter	Has a subject	Has an action	Spelling	Punctuation
☐	☐	☐	☐	☐

Katherine Johnson

Constance Baker Motley

📖 **Read the facts.**

Pronouns: she/her

was born in 1921

died in 2005

was a civil rights activist

was a lawyer

was the first Black woman to serve as a federal judge

✏️ **Write about the person using complete sentences.**

_____

_____

_____

_____

_____

_____

Sentence Writing Checklist

Capital letter	Has a subject	Has an action	Spelling	Punctuation
☐	☐	☐	☐	☐

Constance Baker Motley

_____

_____

_____

_____

_____

_____

_____

_____

Alice Coachman

📖 **Read the facts.**

Pronouns: she/her

was born in 1923

died in 2014

majored in chemistry

invented Kevlar fiber

mentored female scientists

✏️ **Write about the person using complete sentences.**

_____

_____

_____

_____

_____

_____

Sentence Writing Checklist

Capital letter	Has a subject	Has an action	Spelling	Punctuation
☐	☐	☐	☐	☐

Alice Coachman

Alice Coachman

📖 **Read the facts.**

Pronouns: she/her

was born in 1923

died in 2014

picked cotton

was the first Black woman to win an Olympic gold medal

was a teacher

✏️ **Write about the person using complete sentences.**

_____

_____

_____

_____

_____

_____

Sentence Writing Checklist

Capital letter	Has a subject	Has an action	Spelling	Punctuation
☐	☐	☐	☐	☐

Alice Coachman

Dr. Nancy Roman

📖 **Read the facts.**

Pronouns: she/her

was born in 1925

died in 2018

organized an astronomy club as a child

earned a doctorate in astronomy

was NASA's first female executive

✏️ **Write about the person using complete sentences.**

_____

_____

_____

_____

_____

_____

Sentence Writing Checklist

Capital letter	Has a subject	Has an action	Spelling	Punctuation
☐	☐	☐	☐	☐

Dr. Nancy Roman

Margaret Hamilton

📖 **Read the facts.**

Pronouns: she/her

was born in 1936

led the team that wrote the software for the Apollo 11 moon landing

was a computer scientist

was a mother

✏️ **Write about the person using complete sentences.**

_____

_____

_____

_____

_____

_____

Sentence Writing Checklist

Capital letter	Has a subject	Has an action	Spelling	Punctuation
☐	☐	☐	☐	☐

Margaret Hamilton

_____

_____

_____

_____

_____

_____

_____

_____

_____

Wilma Rudolph

📖 **Read the facts.**

Pronouns: she/her

was born in 1940

died in 1994

had polio as a child

wore a leg brace as a child

was a track and field star

✎ **Write about the person using complete sentences.**

_____

_____

_____

_____

_____

_____

Sentence Writing Checklist

Capital letter	Has a subject	Has an action	Spelling	Punctuation
☐	☐	☐	☐	☐

Wilma Rudolph

Sonia Sotomayor

📖 **Read the facts.**

Pronouns: she/her

was born in 1954

was a lawyer

was a judge

was the first Latina, and third woman to serve on the Supreme Court

✏️ **Write about the person using complete sentences.**

_____

_____

_____

_____

_____

_____

Sentence Writing Checklist

Capital letter	Has a subject	Has an action	Spelling	Punctuation
☐	☐	☐	☐	☐

Sonia Sotomayor

_____

_____

_____

_____

_____

_____

_____

_____

Terms of Use

Thank you for purchasing this product.
The contents are the property of Ellie Tiemann and licensed to you only for classroom/personal use as a single user. I retain the copyright, and reserve all rights to this product.

You may not claim this work as your own, giveaway, or sell any portion of this product. You may not share this product anywhere on the internet or on school share sites.

Find more teaching resources at

https://www.teacherspayteachers.com/Store/A-World-Of-Language-Learners

Get weekly tips and find out about teaching resources at

https://www.aworldoflanguagelearners.com/newsletter/